Debbie's Diary

Iris Howden

Published in association with
The Basic Skills Agency

Hodder
A MEMBER OF T

Acknowledgements
Illustrations: Maureen Carter.
Cover: Stephanie Hawken/Organisation.

Orders: please contact Bookpoint Ltd, 39 Milton Park, Abingdon, Oxon OX14
4TD. Telephone: (44) 01235 400414, Fax: (44) 01235 400454. Lines are open
from 9.00–6.00, Monday to Saturday, with a 24 hour message answering service.
Email address: orders@bookpoint.co.uk

British Library Cataloguing in Publication Data
A catalogue record for this title is available from The British Library

ISBN 0 340 72096 4

First published 1998
Impression number   10 9 8 7 6 5 4 3
Year   2002 2001 2000 1999

Typeset by Fakenham Photosetting Ltd, Fakenham, Norfolk.
Printed in Great Britain for Hodder & Stoughton Educational, a division of
Hodder Headline Plc, 338 Euston Road, London NW1 3BH by Athenaeum Press
Ltd, Gateshead, Tyne & Wear.

Debbie's Diary

Contents

1

Meeting Nigel

Tuesday 22 April.

A bad day at work.

Mrs King had a heart attack.

I had been out walking the dogs.

The first thing I saw when I got back

was the ambulance.

Annie shouted to me as it drove off.

'I'm going with her. See you later.'

Old Ted was in the yard.

'What was all that about?' I asked.

'Has someone been hurt?'

'It's the boss,' he said. 'Mrs King.

I think she's had a heart attack.'

'What shall we do?' I asked.

'Carry on as normal,' Ted said.

'I'll give you a hand, Debbie.'

That was nice of him.

Ted is quite old. Over seventy.

He's the handyman really.

He should have retired years ago,

but Mrs King let him stay on.

He lives in the cottage in the grounds.

Keeps an eye on the place at night.

I'd been working at the kennels

since I left school.

I love animals. Dogs most of all.

So the job was made for me.

It's quite a small outfit.

Just Mrs King the owner, Annie and me.

Annie was in charge.

I took my orders from her.

Now I'd have to do my best,

until she got back.

It was after seven before she came.

I should go home at six

but I hung on.

I couldn't leave Ted on his own.

'How is she?' I asked Annie.

'Not too good,' Annie said.

'I think she'll be off work for a while.

I've rung Nigel.

He's coming over tomorrow.'

Nigel was Mrs King's son.

He was her pride and joy.

We had never met him.

Wednesday 23 April.

Met Nigel today. He's really vile.

To think he'll be our boss for weeks. Help!

Nigel was in the office when I got to work.

'You're late,' he said.

It was one minute past eight.

We work a really long day anyway.

I wanted to tell him that

I'd been there 12 hours the day before.

Nigel held out his hand to me.

It was like shaking hands with a jellyfish.

His hand was plump and soft.

Like the rest of him.

Nigel wore a suit and tie.

He had black greasy hair and glasses.

He had a calculator on the desk.

A pile of papers in front of him.

'I'll be in charge for a few weeks,'

he told us.

'My mother will need some time off.

She's been over-doing things.

You two can carry on as normal.'

He went back to his papers.

He wasn't about to help us.

'Is that the famous Nigel?' I asked Annie.

'Looks like it,' Annie said.

She never said much. 'Best get on, OK?'

I was gobsmacked.

We'd never seen Nigel.

From the way Mrs King had gone on

about him I'd been expecting more.

A Brad Pitt look-alike maybe.

A guy with good looks and charm.

A sense of humour at least.

Nigel had none of these.

He was podgy and boring.

He looked like a bank clerk.

He had as much charm as a slug.

We were in for a hard time.

2

Missing Annie

Monday 5 May.

Went to Annie's leaving do on Saturday.

Quite a good night.

Too worn out to write more today.

Nasty Nigel is a real pain.

It was two weeks since Mrs King's

heart attack. Two weeks of hell.

When I first started work I was always tired.

It's a tough job working at a kennel.

Long hours. Lots of effort.

Cleaning, grooming, walking the dogs.

It's not a job for a wimp.

But I wasn't on my own then.

Annie was a hard worker.

She was a big strong girl.

And Mrs King did her share.

She was the boss, but she would

roll her sleeves up if we were busy.

Nasty Nigel thought it was beneath him

to get his hands dirty.

'I'm the brains of the outfit,' he said.

'You need me to do the books.

I've been to business school.'

He didn't know much about dogs.

In fact I think he was scared of them.

He kept well away from them.

He spent his time being smarmy to the owners.

'Of course, madam,' he'd say.

'Little Fluffy (or Rex or Ben)

will get the best of care here.

We aim to please. Parkway Kennels

is a home from home for your pet.'

'Yuck,' Annie said to me.

Which just about summed it up.

Annie was leaving to get married.

Going to live on a croft in Scotland.

She and Grant had been going out

for five years. She didn't rush things.

'Can't you stay on?' I begged her.

'Just till Mrs King gets back?'

'Nope,' she said. 'It's all fixed.

The church is booked.

So's the honeymoon.

I can't let Grant down.'

Her friends weren't going to the wedding.

It was too far away.

We had a party for her instead.

A hen party at the local pub.

'No strip-a-grams,' Annie said.

'No blue jokes. No spiked drinks.'

So we had chicken and chips.

A glass of wine each.

It wasn't what you'd call a rave-up.

But we had a good time.

'I'll miss you a lot,' I told Annie,

crying into my paper napkin.

'Not that much,' Annie said.

'You're just upset because you're

left with Nasty Nigel.'

This was true. I didn't realise

how true until Monday came.

There was no-one else to do the work.

'When's the new person coming,'

I asked.

'Wait until Mother's better,' Nigel said.

'You can manage for a few weeks.'

I could manage. Just about.

With Ted's help I got through the day.

I made sure the dogs' bedding was clean.

Filled their water bowls.

Mucked out the runs.

Then there was the grooming.

Brushing each dog.

And the exercise.

I had hoped Nigel would help.

At least take them for walks.

No such luck.

He stayed in the office,

bent over his calculator.

I began to think he had

a calculator for a heart.

By the time I'd fed the dogs and

ridden home on my bike,

I was too tired to eat.

All I wanted to do was crawl into bed.

I was working a 12-hour day,

seven days a week.

It was a nightmare.

3

A Helping Hand

Friday 23 May.

In trouble again with Nigel, the nerd!

Met the man of my dreams!!!

Things went from bad to worse.

Mrs Collins left Toto for two weeks
while she went to Spain.

Toto was a fat spaniel.

A very fat spaniel.

I felt sorry for him.

He could hardly drag himself around.

I soon found out why.

Before she left, Mrs Collins
handed me Toto's little case.

Inside were his brush and comb.

His own towel with his name on it.

And a stack of chocolate bars.

'Those are his treats,' she said.

'Make sure he gets one every day.'

I looked at Toto. He looked back
at me with his sad brown eyes.

'No more treats for you, Toto,' I said.

'I'm going to get you fit.'

I took Toto out a lot for the
next two weeks.
At first he didn't like it.
He wasn't used to exercise.
One day we got into trouble.
But it led to my meeting Sam
– the man of my dreams.

I had taken Toto and Bess, a collie,
over the fields.
There was a fence on the way back.
Bess jumped up over the fence.
Poor Toto tried but he couldn't jump.
He sat down and waited.
I tried pushing him under the fence.
It was no good. He was still too fat.
Then I tried lifting him over it.
He was far too heavy for me.

I was cross. Now we'd have to go

back the long way. We'd be late.

I'd be in trouble with Nigel.

'Can I help you?'

I looked up and there in front of me

was this great-looking guy.

The man of my dreams.

He was wearing a green waxed jacket.

His dog was pretty neat too.

A red setter in tip-top shape.

'Er, yes, if you could,' I said.

'I can't get Toto over the fence.'

He thought it was funny.

'Hang on to Julius for me,' he said.

He handed me the setter's lead.

Then he heaved Toto over the fence.

'Thanks a lot. You've saved my life,'
I said. 'I'm Debbie, by the way.
I work at Parkway Kennels.'

'My name's Sam,' he said. 'Sam West.
I'm staying with my father.
Maybe I'll see you around?'
'I hope so,' I said under my breath.
Sam West was drop-dead gorgeous.
He was like his dog. Tall and sleek.
It's true what they say.
People do look like their dogs.
Mrs Collins did. She was short and stout.
'If you were a dog,' I once told Annie,
'You'd be a labrador. Big and steady.
A dog you could trust.
What sort would I be?'
'A Jack Russell,' she said. 'Little and nosy.
Now get on with some work.'

I was smiling at the thought of this

when I got back.

Nigel soon wiped the smile off my face.

'Where have you been?' he shouted.

'Mrs Collins is here to collect Toto.'

I had hoped Mrs C. would thank me

for the way I'd got Toto into shape.

No such luck.

'What have you done to my baby?'

she sobbed, seeing the new slim-line Toto.

'He's gone so thin. Poor little darling.'

Nasty Nigel piled on the smarm.

'He's been pining for you, madam,'

he said. 'He wouldn't eat a thing.

He missed you so much.'

This seemed to please the old bat.

She paid up and left.

I waved goodbye to Toto.

He'd done me a big favour,

helping me to meet Sam.

Nigel turned on me.

'What did you do to the little beast?'

he said. 'Starve it?'

'No, of course not,' I said.

I told him how I'd cut out the treats.

Taken Toto for long walks.

'I was getting him fit,' I said.

'All that chocolate was bad for him.

Your mother doesn't let the dogs

have junk food.'

'Mother isn't here,' Nigel said.

'From now on,

the customer is always right.'

Tuesday 3 June.

Sam to the rescue again. He asked me out!

We're going to the cinema on Saturday.

I soon got into trouble again.

This time it could have been serious.

I was still having to do all the work.

Take the dogs out on my own.

I could have left them in the runs.

But they needed some exercise.

I had taken Jip, a corgi, and Bella, a scottie.

I thought I could manage Max too.

Max was a boxer. A young dog.

He was very playful.

Things went OK till we got to the river.

Max loves water. As soon as I took

his lead off, he jumped into the river.

I found a stick to throw for him.

He was having great fun

fetching it out of the water.

Then before I could stop him,

he ran up to some kids.

They were fishing on the bank.

Max was only trying to play.

He wanted them to throw the stick.

But he gave them a fright.

One of them backed away.

He slipped and fell into the river.

I didn't stop to think.

I left the other dogs and went in.

The water wasn't very deep.

But it could have been nasty.

A child could have drowned.

I dragged the boy onto the bank.

He was wet through but not hurt.

'I'm so sorry,' I said. 'Are you OK?'

Then a voice cut in.

'In trouble again Debbie?'

I looked up. Sam was standing there.

'Come on,' he said. 'I'll take you home.'

We packed the kids and the dogs into his jeep.

First we took the boys home to their mum.

Sam drove me home to change.

Then he took me back to the kennels.

I knew I looked a mess.

My hair was hanging in wet strands.

My face and hands were caked with mud.

It took me by surprise when he said,

'Are you doing anything on Saturday?'

'Fancy going to see a film?' he asked.

'Lovely,' I said, hoping I'd be able

to stay awake to see it.

We agreed to meet at seven.

He dropped me at the kennels.

Nosy Nigel came out.

'Who was that?' he asked.

'I hope you're not seeing boyfriends

in working hours.'

That did it. I lost my temper.

I told him how I felt.

I didn't care if it cost me my job.

'I haven't had a single day off since

your mother was taken ill,' I said.

'If you don't get me some help, I'll quit.

You can do everything yourself.'

That worked.

Nigel went pale at the thought

of having to do some hard work.

'Don't be like that, Debbie,' he said.

'Of course I'll get someone in.

A girl called the other day.

A schoolgirl wanting a part-time job.

I'll give her a ring right away.'

So Mandy started to work for us.

She came after school and at weekends.

It made my life a lot better.

I was able to get off early on Saturday.

To get ready for my date.

4

A Nasty Incident

Thursday 12 June.

Saturday was great, but today was
the worst day of my life. Fell out with Sam.

At the start of June, Jed Marvin
brought his dogs in. Jed was a pop star.
He'd been really big in the 1980s.

He had this huge house in its own grounds.

He kept two guard dogs and let them

run loose at night.

They were Dobermans. Really mean dogs.

They'd bite if you weren't careful.

Jed left them when he went on tour.

I dreaded them. They're the only dogs

I've ever been scared of.

Even Mrs King was wary of them.

'Don't take them out together,' she told me.

'They act like pack animals.'

I had one of them on the lead

when Nigel came out.

'Make sure these dogs are well looked after.

People know Jed Marvin's dogs board here.

It could be good for business,' he said.

'Aren't you taking the other one as well?'

'No,' I said. 'Your mum told me

never to take them out together.'

'Don't waste time taking just one dog,'

he said. 'Take them both.'

'But they run wild,' I said.

'Rubbish,' Nigel the know-all said.

'Just keep them well under control.'

'Nigel, they can be dangerous,' I said.

But it was no good. Nigel knew best.

'Don't argue with me,' he said.

'And it's Mr King to you.'

'Yes, Mr King,' I said in a sarcastic way.

I felt like calling him 'Your majesty'.

But I didn't dare. I had got on

the wrong side of Nigel too often.

I took the hounds from hell to a quiet spot.

I didn't dare risk taking them by the river.

There were children playing there.

People walking their dogs.

The Dobermans might start a fight.

They pulled on the lead all the time.

'Heel,' I kept shouting but it was no use.

Then I saw Sam coming with Julius.

'Sam,' I shouted, 'Go back. Keep away.'

He didn't hear me.

He kept walking towards us. He waved.

The Dobermans went mad.

They were big strong dogs.

They pulled me over.

As I fell I let go of the leads.

They were off like two black streaks.

Running towards Sam's dog.

They ran round Julius barking.

Then they went for him.

Sam waved his stick at them.

Before he could stop them, they closed in.

They bit Julius on the neck and back.

Sam had to ward them off with his stick.

By the time I got there he had got

them under control.

He had tied their leads to the fence.

Poor Julius was lying on the grass.

Blood was pouring from him.

Sam knelt by his side.

His face was white with rage.

'You stupid girl!' he shouted at me.

'How could you let those dogs go?

Look what they've done to Julius.'

I tried to explain. To tell him how

Nigel made me bring them.

But it was no good.

'Get them away from here,' he said.

'I need to ring the vet.'

He got out his mobile phone.

I walked away in tears.

By now the Dobermans were quiet.

Sadly, I took them back to the kennels.

It was all over between me and Sam.

What had started so well had ended badly.

Our date on Saturday had been great.

Now it might never have been.

Sam had spoken to me like a stranger.

Later I saw him park his jeep in the yard.

Nigel called me into the office.

'What's all this about Mr West's dog
being attacked,' he said.
'Julius is a top show dog.
How could you let it happen?'
'Mr King,' I said. 'I did try to tell you.
Your mother told me not to take those
dogs out together.'
'I didn't hear you say that,' Nigel lied.
'I'm very sorry, Mr West.
The girl will have to pay the vet's bill.'

'Don't try to put the blame on your staff,'
Sam said. 'You own the kennels.
It's down to you.
I'll send you the bill.
It won't do your business much good
if people hear about this.'

'No, of course not,' Nigel said. 'I agree.

Your bill will be paid in full.

I'm really sorry.'

He went on in his usual creepy way.

'You can go now, Debbie,' he told me.

Sam came to find me in the yard.

'I'm sorry I yelled at you,' he said.

'I was upset. It seems Julius is OK.

The vet said they were only flesh wounds.

Nigel should never have made you take

those dogs out. I've told him that.

You won't get into any trouble.'

'Do you know Nigel then?' I asked.

'From way back,' Sam said.

'We were at school together.

He was a little creep then.

I met him again at business school.

So I know what he's like.

I don't blame you Debbie.

How about a drink later to show

there's no hard feelings?'

5

Things are Looking up

Tuesday 1 July.

Mrs King is back at work.

A new month. A new job. A new boss.

Mrs King came in to work this week.

There was no sign of Nigel.

I was hoping things would be back
to normal at last.
Mrs King asked me into the office.
She made me a coffee.
'Sit down, Debbie,' she said.
'I want to talk to you.'

'First of all let me say thank-you.
I know how hard you've worked
while I've been away.
It can't have been easy for you.'
'Who told you that?' I said.
I couldn't see Nigel putting in
a good word for me.
'I've been speaking to Ted,' Mrs King said.
'He has worked for me for many years.
I know I can take his word.
Let me get straight to the point.

I'd like to offer you Annie's job.

You will be in charge.

It will mean a rise in wages.

What do you say?'

'Yes, please,' I said.

I just about got the words out.

'How do you feel about having Mandy

as your assistant?' Mrs King asked.

'She's due to leave school soon.'

'That would be great,' I said.

'Mandy's a good worker,

and we get on well.'

'My doctor told me to take things easy,'
Mrs King said.

'So I'm putting a manager in charge.
But I'll still pop in from time to time.'

'A manager?' My heart sank.
I feared the worst.

'Do you mean Nigel?' I asked.

'No, not Nigel.' Mrs King said.

'Nigel's not really a doggy person.'
It was the nearest she'd get to saying
anything bad about her darling son.

'Nigel's better on the money side.

He wants to go out to America.

Work there for a year or two.'

'What a good idea!' I said,

trying not to sound too pleased.

I was quite happy at the thought of

3,000 miles between me and Nigel.

'But who's going to take over?'

'The son of a local man I know,'

Mrs King went on.

'Sam West. His father came to see me

a few times when I was in hospital.

He said Sam was looking for a job.

Sam was at business school with Nigel.

And he really loves dogs too.

He's helped his father breed the red setters.

I'm sure you two will get on well.'

'I'm sure we will,' I said.

No more nasty Nigel.

I couldn't wait to meet my new boss.

Things were looking up.